FRUIT BAT

First published 1992 by
PAN MACMILLAN CHILDREN'S BOOKS

A division of Pan Macmillan Limited
Cavaye Place, London SW10 9PG
Associated companies throughout the world

Picturemac edition published 1994

A CIP catalogue record for this book is available
from the British Library

Printed in Hong Kong

ISBN 0 333 59305 7

FRUIT BAT

MARK FOREMAN

M

PAN MACMILLAN
CHILDREN'S BOOKS

One day a large wooden crate arrived at the Botanical gardens . . . but what was in it?

When the garden keepers opened the crate
a small furry animal flew out!

It flew straight up and hid in the top of the glasshouse.
It was a fruit bat.

She was very hungry after her long journey
in the crate and her sharp eyes soon saw some
ripe bananas growing down below.

Suddenly there was a lot of shouting.

"Hey, leave our bananas alone!" cried the
keepers and they chased her with their big nets.

The frightened fruit bat escaped back to
the safety of the roof. There she stayed for the
rest of the day and through the night.

She was now feeling hungrier than ever!

The next day, a group of children came into the
glasshouse with their teacher, Miss Match. They
sat round the lily pond and opened their lunch boxes.

"Mmmmm!" thought Fruit Bat, "that smells delicious."

Fruit Bat flew down and settled near a little boy.
He was startled at first, but he liked her
upside-down grin and offered her a sandwich.

Fruit Bat took a mighty bite . . .

She immediately began to cough and splutter.
That was not the food for her!

Miss Match pointed out that fruit bats would
prefer fruit to a cheese and onion sandwich.

Meanwhile . . .

when the keeper leapt out with his big net
the children jumped up in surprise and their
food flew everywhere! Fruit Bat took off
once more, high up into the roof.

Fruit Bat knew that she could not stay there
for ever. The keepers didn't want her to damage
the rare plants, and anyway there was not enough
food for her. So, as the children were leaving,
she flew down and out through the doors
just before they were closed.

Outside it was very different.

"This place is not like home," Fruit Bat thought.
"It's not very hot – and where are the fruit trees?"

It began to get dark, and colder. Fruit Bat,
looking for shelter, flew to a strange-looking
tall building. She found a snug corner, high up
and out of the wind and she began to doze.

Suddenly she was woken by lots of screeching
and squawking.

"Clear off, clear off! We don't want funny-
looking birds like you around here!
Go back to where you came from!"

A mob of scruffy old pigeons beat her with their
wings and tried to peck her with their beaks.

Poor Fruit Bat flew off into the night feeling
sad and hurt. At last, she came to a tree
in which she could rest.

Next day, as the sun rose, the hungry fruit bat
explored the gardens, looking for food.

Late that afternoon, Fruit Bat heard the sound
of laughter. Another group of children were
about to leave the gardens.

Fruit Bat flew down and settled on the roof-rack
of the school bus.

Just before it arrived at the school, the bus
drove through a busy street market. Fruit Bat
was amazed by all the brightly coloured things
that were for sale.

But one stall in particular caught her eye . . .
the fruit stall! Even Fruit Bat had never seen
so many different kinds of fruit before.

"Look, Miss Match, there's a funny-looking
bird hanging from our bus!" cried Sam.

"That's the fruit bat I saw yesterday," said
Miss Match. "They come from very hot
countries with forests full of fruit trees and animals.
She must be very lonely here all by herself."

"Can we look after her, Miss?" asked Lottie hopefully.

"Well," said Miss Match, "perhaps we could build
a home for her to stay in."

So that afternoon Miss Match showed the children how to build a bat-box. They hung it in a sheltered corner of the playground where they could watch it from their classrooms.

Miss Match and the children bought some fruit
from the market to tempt Fruit Bat into her
new home.

It worked – and Fruit Bat settled in.

The next day, the fruit-stall owner took a basket
of fruit to the school and invited the fruit bat
to visit his stall at any time.

People came from far and wide to see the fruit stall which had its own fruit bat.

"You can eat as much as you like, Fruit Bat," said the owner, "and maybe you will even get used to the weather. I did."

Also available by Mark Foreman

SCRAPS
SID THE KITTEN

Other Picturemacs you will enjoy

MUCKY MOOSE   Jonathan Allen
ONE BEAR IN HOSPITAL   Caroline Bucknall
GUMBOOT'S CHOCOLATEY DAY   Mick Inkpen
BUSHBABY   Adrienne Kennaway
THE WIZARD, THE FAIRY AND THE MAGIC CHICKEN   Helen Lester/Lynn Munsinger
IF DINOSAURS WERE CATS AND DOGS   Colin McNaughton
MRS PIG'S BULK BUY   Mary Rayner
MY GRAMPA HAS BIG POCKETS   Selina Young

For a complete list of Picturemac titles write to

Pan Macmillan Children's Books
18–21 Cavaye Place London SW10 9PG